Mais Oui, Marie

CREOLE COOKIN'

Life and Flavor in the Creole Tradition

A Cookbook filled with
Authentic Creole Recipes and Stories by
MARIE LASTRAPES

Compiled and Edited by
ANITA PORCHÉ

Illustrations by
ANTHONY WIMBERLY

Story Editing by
NAN MITCHELL

Proof Editing by
RUTH CAMBRE

Special thanks to all who helped to make this publication possible ... especially my husband, Melvin; our children, Ann and her husband Bobby Porché and Melvin, Jr. and his wife Bobbie Lastrapes; and our granddaughter, Anita Porché. Thank you for your love and support.

Also, special thanks to Ruth Cambre, Nan Mitchell, and to Betty Lavergne and Philip Andrepont of Andrepont Printing, Inc. for your time and effort in helping to make this project a reality.

1ST EDITION
May 1999
ISBN 0-9672043-0-5

TABLE OF CONTENTS

COOKBOOK CORRECTIONS

Page 9	Biscuits-**Shortening**-½ Cup
Page 17	Brandy Lemon Sauce-**Water**-½ cup
Page 26	Calf's Liver-**Garlic**-2 Pods-not 2lbs
Page 31	Meatballs-**Salt & Pepper to Taste**
Page 34	Pie Crust for Meat Pies-**Flour** 5 lbs.
Page 40	Peanut Brittle-**Sugar**-11/4
Page 50	Auntie's Pound Cake-**Butter** -don't melt-**Soften**
Page 51	Date Nut Bread-**Flour**-2 cups

Web Address http://creolerecipes.crazygator.com

3

RECIPE FOR HAPPINESS

Recipe By: Bobby Porche
Serving Size: 1

1 cup good thoughts
1 cup kind deeds
1 cup consideration

2 cups sacrifice for others
3 cups forgiveness
2 cups well beaten faults

Mix thoroughly and add teaspoon of Joy, Sorrow and Sympathy. Flavor with little gifts of love. Fold in 5 cups of prayer and faith to lighten all other ingredients and raise texture to great heights of character. After pouring all this into your daily life, bake well with heat of human kindness. Serve this often.

Serving Ideas : Serve with a smile and will satisfy the hunger of the soul.

AN INTRODUCTION

I would like to introduce my grandmother, Marie Lastrapes, undeniably the best cook in Acadiana (Southwest Louisiana). At one time or another most in the area have had the pleasure to attend a function she has catered. They know, like I know, good Creole cooking doesn't get any better than this.

Marie's Catering of Opelousas, Louisiana has been in business for over 15 years. She has catered for mayors, governors, the "who's who," brides-to-be, and better yet, all who she considers friends and family. Satisfaction is always guaranteed and I can guarantee you that you will be satisfied!

Have you ever seen a cook never measure and always get it right? I have! Have you tasted food that was perfectly delicious as well as perfectly presented? I have! As a little girl, I've had the pleasure of working with her into the wee hours of the night to help prepare for her customers' special occasions. She cooks with love and respect and by the reaction of those who taste her food, it shows!

As a teenager, I remember working those 18 hour days, cleaning up after a wedding or special occasion and my MaMa putting on her dancing shoes with my Dad and going to a Zydeco at Slim's Y-Ki-Ki or Richard's Club. The rest of the house would be dead tired! She truly is the hardest working woman I know... the fountain of youth...an inspiration.

We have put together this cookbook of recipes that represent the culture of our people – the Creole people of Southwest Louisiana. Some of the recipes might include cuts of meat you may have never used before...cheaper cuts of meat creatively prepared in a different way (smothered, stewed, etc.) ... but to Creole people, it's our way. It will also include dishes we would use at weddings, showers, family reunions, Sunday dinners, etc. In Louisiana, we take pride in sharing delicious food with friends and family. It's our way of caring and in some small way, healing. So when you come down, don't be surprised if all we want to do is feed you.

MaMa, I wish you all the success and blessings. You are one divine lady who deserves it. For all of you who own this cookbook, you will treasure it always.

Marie's oldest granddaughter,

Lady

Anita Porché, AKA "Lady"

We grew up in a house exactly like this one.
My brothers would climb the outside stairs to
sleep at night.

COTTON PICKIN' TIME

It's those golden days of an Indian Summer. The sun has not completely risen as the whole family and friends head to those cotton fields, white with promise. Breakfast of native figs and biscuits will come later when the sun has begun to dance in the sky. It's a happy time; those ole favorites, Come, Holy Spirit, and Swing Low Sweet Chariot are being sung. The cotton bags will follow the pickers as they make their way through the rows of cotton.

Later, there will be a long trail of wagons as the cotton is brought to the gin. The cotton will be weighed and then Papa will reward each child with a penny for each pound picked.

After the day's work, when the sun sinks low into the sky, the aroma from the wood-burning stove greets the pickers. It will tell that the day's work is over, and the cotton pickin' has been well done. Marie has included some of those old recipes that are still rewarding.

MARIE'S FIG PRESERVES

Serving Size: 10

2 gallons fresh figs
3 pounds sugar

1 medium lemon - sliced and seeded

Wash figs in cold water with 2 or 3 spoons of baking soda. Then rinse in a second plain water. Put in heavy pot with sugar and lemon slices. Cook on medium heat until syrup is heavy. Takes about 1 hour. I put mine in plastic containers for freezing. They do well! Serving Ideas: Great over toast for breakfast.

BREAKFAST CASSEROLE

Serving Size: 6

1 dozen eggs
16 ounces sour cream
1/4 cup milk
6 medium English muffins

8 ounces cheddar cheese, shredded
1 can green chiles
1 small jar pimento
1 pound roll breakfast sausage
   (Pork) - browned and drained

Cover bottom of a rectangular baking pan with English muffins; split. Beat together eggs, sour cream and milk. Season to taste; salt, black and cayenne pepper. Pour this mixture over muffins. Top with shredded cheese, sausage, green chiles and pimento; in this order. Bake at 375 degrees for 25 - 35 minutes or until knife inserted comes out clean. Serving Ideas: Serve as a holiday brunch.

MY DAD'S EGGS & RICE

Recipe By: MY FATHER
Serving Size: 4

4 medium eggs
3 tablespoons milk
1 cup rice - cooked
3 stalks green onions,
   tops & bottoms - chopped

Beat eggs, milk, and green onions in bowl, season to taste. Add to hot oil in skillet like you would an omelet. Partially cook eggs then stir in rice and scramble. My granddaughter "Lady" (Anita Porché), adds Tabasco. Um Um Good!

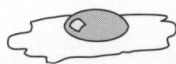

"My Poppa would fix this for his 15 kids on Friday. In those days we didn't eat meat on Fridays. Love you, Poppa." Marie

MY GOOD RICH BISCUITS

Serving Size: 10

2 cups all-purpose flour
4 teaspoons baking powder
1/2 teaspoon salt

3 teaspoons sugar
1/2 cups shortening
2/3 cup whole milk

Sift together dry ingredients. Cut in shortening and add milk. Stir until a soft dough is formed. Turn out on floured surface. Knead and roll about 1/4 inch thick. Use cutter to form biscuits. Bake in a 350 degree oven 10 - 15 minutes. Serving Ideas: Serve with scrambled eggs and bacon.

MARIE'S CRACKLIN' CRUMB CORNBREAD

Serving Size: 12

2 cups yellow cornmeal
1 cup all-purpose flour
3 tablespoons baking powder
2 tablespoons sugar
3 medium eggs

2 tablespoons salt
1 cup crumbs from cracklins
3 tablespoons oil
3 tablespoons sour cream
1 1/2 cups milk

Mix the above ingredients well. Pour into a 9 x 9 x 2 inch baking pan with 2 tablespoons of oil in the bottom of the pan. Bake for about 30 minutes at 350 degrees. Serving Ideas: Very good with mustard greens or cabbage.

MARIE'S PLAIN CORNBREAD

Serving Size: 10

2 cups yellow cornmeal
1 cup all-purpose flour - sifted
4 tablespoons baking powder
3 tablespoons sugar

1 teaspoon salt
1/2 cup oil
1 1/2 cups milk
4 eggs

Mix all the above ingredients well. Use a 9 x 12 x 2 inch pan, spray with Pam and put 3 tablespoons of oil in pan. Pour batter in pan and spoon some oil from the corners on batter. Bake at 350 degrees for about 30 minutes. Serving Ideas: Crumble and add milk...as a cereal.

RED BEANS & RICE

Serving Size: 10

1 pound red kidney beans
2 pounds ham or smoked ham hocks
1 medium onion - chopped
1 medium bell pepper - chopped

2 pods garlic - minced
1 stalk celery - chopped
5 cups water

Put beans to cooking in the 5 cups of water. In another pot, boil the ham hocks for about 1 hour, then put into the beans. Also put the rest of the seasoning (add more water if needed). Let cook until beans are tender. Add salt and cayenne to taste, 15 minutes before turning beans off. Secret ingredient: add 4 tablespoons of catsup. Serving Ideas: Serve over white rice.

MEATBALL STEW

Serving Size: 10

1 pound ground beef
1 pound ground pork
1 small onion - chopped
1 small bell pepper - chopped

3 pods garlic - chopped fine
1/2 cup bread crumbs - soaked
1/2 cup roux

Season meat with salt and black pepper and/or cayenne pepper to taste. Mix all ingredients well, except roux. Form into balls and brown on each side in a little oil. When the meatballs are browned, add the roux and enough water to cover the meatballs. Cover and let simmer for about 30 minutes. Stir every once in a while. Serving Ideas: Serve over rice.

SAUSAGE IN RED GRAVY

Serving Size: 10

2 pounds sausage,
   cut in pieces 4 inches long
1 medium onion - chopped
1 medium bell pepper - chopped
1 stalk celery - chopped

1 small can crushed tomatoes
1 small can tomato paste
1/2 stick butter or margarine
1 cup water
2 pods garlic -chopped

Salt and pepper to taste, go easy. Cut sausage in 4 inch links, put aside. Saute all the other ingredients, then add sausage and 1 cup of water. Cover and cook on low heat for 30 minutes. Serving Ideas: Serve over rice with a green salad.

MARIE'S SMOTHERED GIBLETS

Serving Size: 4

2 pounds giblets-cleaned & boiled
1 small onion - chopped
1 small bell pepper - chopped
2 pods garlic - chopped

1 bunch green onions - chopped
1 tablespoon parsley flakes
1 stick butter or margarine

Clean and boil giblets for 1 hour on a low heat, season water. Melt butter or margarine in heavy pot, add 2 tablespoons flour and stir constantly until it gets to a golden color. Then add giblets and all other ingredients, mix well and add 1 cup of water. Cover and let cook for about 30 minutes. Serve over rice. Serving Ideas: Very good over rice.

MARIE'S TRIPE RECIPE

Serving Size: 8

5 pounds tripe
3 pods garlic - chopped
1 medium onion - chopped

1 medium bell pepper - chopped
1/2 gallon water

Wash well. Place all ingredients in pot, season with salt and pepper to taste. Cook on low heat for about 1 hour or until tender. Serving ideas: Serve with vinegar or reduce water and serve over rive.

DOWN SOUTH CUSH CUSH

Serving Size: 10

2 cups yellow cornmeal
2 teaspoons salt
1 teaspoon baking powder
1 cup milk
1/4 cup oil

Mix cornmeal, salt, baking powder, milk and pour into hot oil in a cast iron pot on the stove. Stir constantly until done. Some call this cornbread on the stove. It cooks very quickly. Serving Ideas: Serve hot with milk like cereal. My grandchildren add sugar.

"My Poppa was disabled and many nights we ate cush cush and milk for supper, but we were happy!"

11

I BELIEVE

It is Ash Wednesday, and the Lenten Season begins with ashes traced in the form of the cross on the forehead of the Roman Catholic. Marie kneels, head covered, as the priest reminds her of the sacrifice of the Lord and the demise of life on this earth. How well she remembers her stepmother's devotion to the cross. On Good Friday, when it wasn't possible to attend Mass, a white cloth was placed over a chair, a crucifix was placed on the chair, and all knelt before the crucifix and kissed the feet of Jesus. This observance was known as "Adoration of the Cross."

Marie's mind wandered back to those Sabbaths when her stepmother awoke sleepy-eyed children at three-thirty in the morning for a buggy ride over dirt roads in order for confession and to attend Mass.

As her father or a brother drove home, a quiet and happy peace could be observed. And to celebrate this day of rest, a gracious meal would be awaiting these Christians. Most of the menu had been prepared the previous day as all forms of work must cease on the Sabbath. Now, bow your heads in thanksgiving, love, and commitment. These recipes tell of all three.

HOT PEPPER JELLY

Recipe By: ANN
Serving Size: 100

3/4 cup bell peppers - ground
1/4 cup hot peppers - ground
5 1/2 cups sugar

1 1/2 cups apple cider vinegar
1 small bottle Certo

Seed and grind peppers in food processor. Save the juice and mix with vinegar and sugar. Bring to full rolling boil - boil about 5 minutes. Add peppers, cook 2 minutes. Cool 5 minutes, then add Certo. Bring to full rolling boil for 1 minute. Cool about 5 minutes and skim top. Put in jelly glasses and seal with paraffin. Wear rubber gloves when handling hot peppers.

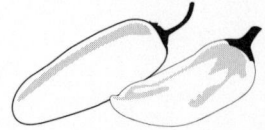

PICKLED PEPPERS

Serving Size: 50

2 large mirlitons (vegetable pear)
1/2 pod of garlic - quartered
1 teaspoon salt

2 cups vinegar
4 medium green tomato wedges
   hot peppers

Peel mirlitons, slice in wedges. Place mirlitons, hot peppers, green tomato wedges on flat pan, lay a cloth over them and place ice sprinkled with salt for a few minutes. Place alternately in quart size jar. Add garlic and salt to vinegar and heat vinegar to boiling point and pour over vegetables. Serving Ideas: Serve with main Creole dishes, especially gumbo.

MARIE'S CHEESE GRITS

Serving Size: 6

1 cup yellow grits
4 cups water
1 teaspoon salt
1 roll garlic cheese

1 stick butter
3 large eggs - beaten well
1/2 cup milk

Add water and salt to a large pot. Cook grits as normal. When cooked, mix in the garlic cheese, butter, milk, eggs, and pepper to taste. Place in a casserole dish and bake in 350 degree oven for 30 - 40 minutes. Wonderful for a brunch! Serving Ideas: Serve with ham, sausage, scrambled eggs and fruit.

MARIE'S SPOON BREAD

Serving Size: 15

2 cups milk
1 cup yellow cornmeal
1 teaspoon salt

4 tablespoons sugar
6 medium eggs - separate out yolks
2 sticks butter

Melt butter in milk. Bring to a boil. Stir in cornmeal and add salt gradually. Let cool. Add egg yolks one at a time. Fold in stiffly beaten egg whites. Bake in a deep Pyrex dish or Corning dish appr. 45 minutes in a moderate oven (350 degrees). Serving Ideas: Very good with corn beef and cabbage.

BOBBIE'S TAHITIAN FRUIT SALAD

Recipe By: BOBBIE LASTRAPES
Serving Size: 8 - 10

8 ounces sour cream
30 ounces fruit cocktail
    drained

1 bag of small marshmallows, colored
1 small can coconut

Mix all of the above ingredients and chill 4 - 6 hours. Serve as a salad or as a dessert. Serving Ideas: Serve on lettuce cups (whole leaf).

HARVEY HOUSE SLAW

Serving Size: 8

1 large cabbage head - thinly sliced
1 large white onion - cut in rings
1/4 cup sugar
1 teaspoon dry mustard
1 teaspoon celery seed

1 cup white vinegar
1 teaspoon salt
3/4 cup salad oil
1 small green bell pepper
    chopped

In large mixing bowl, make layers of cabbage, green pepper and onion. Sprinkle sugar on top. In saucepan combine mustard, 2 teaspoons of sugar, the celery seeds, salt, vinegar and oil, then bring to a full boil, pour over slaw. Refrigerate covered at least 4 hours. Toss when ready to serve. Serving Ideas: Great for a picnic or barbecue.

MRS. BROWN'S CURRIED FRUIT

Recipe By: MRS. BROWN
Serving Size: 20

1 large can pears - drained
1 large can peach halves
  drained - cut in chunks
1 large can pineapple chunks
  in juice - drained

3 medium bananas - mashed
1 1/2 teaspoons curry powder
2 sticks butter - melted
1/2 cup sugar
2 teaspoons cinnamon

Melt the butter and add the curry, put aside. Mix the sugar with the cinnamon and put aside. Layer half the fruit in baking dish and pour half the butter mixture on top. Put second layer and pour the balance of the butter mixture. Top with the sugar mixture, then bake in a 350 degree oven for appr. 35 minutes. Serving Ideas: Great for a brunch.

RUTH'S VEGETABLE SOUP

Recipe By: MRS. RUTH CAMBRE
Serving Size: 12

2 gallons water - boiled
4 pounds round roast or similar
  meat - cut in 1/2 inch squares
12 ounces tomato paste
4 stalks celery - sliced
1 large onion - chopped

1/2 medium bell pepper - chopped
1 med. head of cabbage - sliced
  thin
1/2 pound frozen corn
1/2 pound frozen mixed vegetables
1/2 pound carrots - sliced
1 small package egg noodles

Note: Don't cut down on the cabbage as it is the base of the soup and does not end up tasting like a cabbage dish.
Combine first seven ingredients in large deep pot and season with salt, black pepper, cayenne to taste. Add Worcestershire sauce. Cook at a low boil appr. 4 hours, adding water as needed. Add frozen corn, mixed vegetables, carrots, and noodles. Cook an additional 30 minutes or until vegetables are cooked. Recheck seasoning and serve. Serving Ideas: Serve with crackers.

POPPA'S 1930'S BEEF & VEGETABLE SOUP

Recipe By: MY DAD
Serving Size: 15

5 pounds soup bones
3 medium carrots - cut
1/2 small cabbage - chopped

3 med. turnips - cut in small cubes
1 cup rice or pasta
1 can tomato paste

He would put the meat to boiling in a heavy pot. When almost tender, he would add the vegetables, rice or pasta and salt and pepper. Let cook another half hour. Serving Ideas: Serve with crackers.

Now, instead of rice, I put pasta in my soup and I also put potatoes. In those days we didn't know much about pasta.

"Every Sunday, after Mass, my Poppa would cook soup for us."

MARIE'S CREOLE BREAD PUDDING

Serving Size: 10

1 large loaf of French bread,
  stale - broken up
1 small angel food cake
  broken up
1 quart milk
1 stick butter
6 large eggs

2 cups sugar
1/2 cup white raisins
1 teaspoon vanilla extract
3 tablespoons flour
1 large egg yolk
1/4 cup brandy
1/4 cup lemon juice

BREAD PUDDING

Break bread into small pieces and soak in the milk. Beat eggs in 1 cup of sugar and 2 tablespoons of flour, add raisins and vanilla. Add this mixture to the bread and milk, mix well. Break angel food cake into small chunks and add to the above mixture. Let soak over night in refrigerator. When ready to bake, melt butter in deep 9 x 13 inch pan and pour bread pudding mixture over butter and bake in 300 degree oven for 1 hour.

BRANDY LEMON SAUCE

Mix 1 tablespoon flour, the water, 1 egg yolk and 1 cup of sugar, in a small pot. Let come to a boil. Cook until thick, remove from heat and add brandy and lemon juice. Pour over bread pudding. Serving Ideas: Great for a dinner party, served hot.

17

MARIE'S CHEESE SQUARES

Serving Size: 30

1 box yellow cake mix
1 stick butter - softened
4 medium eggs
1 teaspoon vanilla extract

8 ounces cream cheese
1 box powdered sugar
1/2 cup lemon juice

<u>Step 1</u> - Crust: Mix yellow cake mix, butter, 1 egg and vanilla extract until crumbly. Spread in 9 x 13 inch baking pan. Flour hands and spread mixture from center to edge evenly. <u>Step 2</u>: Beat cream cheese, 3 eggs, lemon juice, and powdered sugar well. Pour into crust. Bake 30 - 40 minutes at 375 degrees. Let cool, cut into small squares. Serving Ideas: Holiday dessert.

NAN'S LOUISIANA HURRICANE CAKE

Recipe By: NAN
Serving Size: 15

1 1/2 cups sugar
2 medium eggs
3 cups fruit cocktail in juice
2 tablespoons baking soda
2 cups flour
1/4 cup brown sugar
1 cup pecans - chopped

TOPPING
1 stick butter
3/4 cup sugar
1/2 cup evaporated milk
1 cup coconut

CAKE

Mix and cream together sugar, eggs, fruit cocktail, baking soda and flour. Pour into lightly greased and floured 13 x 9 x 2 inch pan. Mix brown sugar and nuts and sprinkle onto the unbaked batter in the pan. Bake in 350 degree oven for 45 minutes.

TOPPING

Heat butter - when it gets to a boil, add 3/4 cup of sugar and 1/2 cup evaporated milk and cook for 12 minutes or more. Add 1 cup coconut to mixture and spoon over cake fresh out of the oven.

BAKED MACARONI & CHEESE

Recipe By: ELOUISE
Serving Size: 8

12 ounce package of macaroni
1 large can Carnation milk

1 stick butter or margarine
1/2 pound cheese - grated

Boil macaroni and drain, put back in boiling pot. Add milk, cheese, butter or margarine, and add salt and pepper to taste. Stir. Spray baking dish with Pam and pour mixture in dish. Bake in 350 degree oven about 45 minutes or until medium brown.

LOUISIANA STYLE BAKED BEANS

Serving Size: 12

6 slices bacon
1 gallon pork and beans
1 cup catsup
1 cup brown sugar

1/2 cup onion - chopped
1/2 cup bell pepper - chopped
2 tablespoons dry mustard

Drain beans well. Mix all the above ingredients well, except bacon. Pour in Pyrex dish sprayed with Pam. Lay slices of bacon on top. Cover and bake 20 minutes, then uncover and bake 20 minutes longer.

MARIE'S CREAMED CABBAGE

Serving Size: 15

1 medium head of cabbage
  chopped and steamed
1 1/2 sticks butter
1/2 cup all-purpose flour

1 1/2 cups milk
1/2 pound Velvetta cheese - cubed
1 cup sharp or mild cheddar cheese
  shredded

Melt butter in heavy pot, add flour and let come to a bubble. Don't let it brown. Add milk and Velvetta cheese, season to taste. (Easy on the salt.) Pour over cabbage and sprinkle 1 cup grated sharp or mild cheese over cabbage. Bake in a 350 degree oven until bubbling hot. *I was told several times that people who didn't like cabbage ate this and liked it.* Serving Ideas: Serve with any meal.

SHRIMP CREOLE

Serving Size: 10

2 pounds shrimp
  peeled and de-veined
1 medium onion - chopped
1 stalk celery - chopped
1 medium bell pepper- chopped
2 pods garlic - chopped fine
1 can tomatoes - chopped

1 bunch green onions
  cut into thin slivers
2 tablespoons flour
2 1/2 cups water
2 sticks butter
1 small can tomato paste
1/4 cup parsley - chopped

Melt butter in heavy pot, add flour, onions, bell peppers and garlic. Saute this until wilted. Add tomatoes and tomato paste and cook approximately 45 minutes. Season to taste. Then add shrimp and water. Reduce to low fire, simmer for appr. 20 minutes. Top off with chopped parsley and green onions to add pizazz. Bon Appetit!

MARIE'S CORN MACQUE CHOUX

Serving Size: 10

3 14-ounce cans whole
  kernel corn - drained
1 14-ounce can cream style corn
1 small onion - chopped
1/2 medium bell pepper - chopped

2 large red tomatoes
  peeled and chopped
1 tablespoon sugar
1 stick butter

Melt butter and add all of the above ingredients and cook on medium fire for appr. 15 minutes. Season to taste.

MARIE'S SWEET POTATO CRUNCH

Serving Size: 12

3 large sweet potatoes
2/3 cup sugar
1 teaspoon salt
4 medium eggs - beaten
1 stick butter
1 teaspoon vanilla flavoring

TOPPING
1 cup brown sugar
2/3 cup oatmeal
2 tablespoons flour
2/3 stick butter
1 cup pecans

Parboil potatoes, peel and cube in 1/2 inch squares and place in casserole dish. Combine sugar, salt, beaten eggs, butter and vanilla. Pour over potatoes.
For Topping, add remaining ingredients to the melted butter and sprinkle over the casserole. Bake at 350 degrees for appr. 35 minutes. Serving Ideas: Serve hot with a meal.

MARIE'S SMOTHERED OKRA

Serving Size: 10

2 pounds okra - sliced
1 small onion - chopped
1 small bell pepper - chopped
2 pods garlic - chopped fine

1 8-ounce can crushed tomatoes
 (Hunt's)
4 tablespoon oil

Heat oil in heavy pot (not in a black iron pot), and add all the above ingredients. Mix well. Season to taste. Stay with it because it will burn easily. When it smothers down good, add about 1/2 cup water and let simmer a few minutes. Don't overcook. Chicken or shrimp may be added, if desired.

SWEET PEAS IN BUTTER SAUCE

Serving Size: 8

2 cans peas, 303
1/2 cup cream of mushroom soup

1/2 stick butter
2 tablespoons sugar

Drain peas. Put all ingredients in a pot, add black pepper to taste, and heat That's it!

COLE SLAW

Serving Size: 10

1 medium cabbage - shredded
1 can pineapple chunks in juice
3 tablespoons sugar

1/2 cup salad dressing
1/4 cup Italian dressing

Mix salt, black pepper (to taste), sugar and the dressings all together. Pour over cabbage and pineapple. Toss well. Put in a covered Tupperware bowl and let chill overnight, if possible. Serving Ideas: Great with any meal.

MARIE'S FAMOUS CORNBREAD DRESSING

Serving Size: 15

2 cups yellow cornmeal
1 cup all-purpose flour
2 teaspoons salt
4 tablespoons baking powder
2 tablespoons sugar

5 medium eggs
2 cups milk*
1/3 cup oil
1 cup herb-seasoned bread crumbs

Heat oil in the baking pan that you will use for the cornbread. Mix all the above ingredients well, except for the bread crumbs, and pour the hot oil in the mixture. Pour another 1/3 cup of oil in the bottom of the pan and pour mixture onto it. Bake in a 350 degree oven for about 30 minutes. When done, cool and crumble, and add herb-seasoned bread crumbs. Set aside. *P.S. I use the dry milk instead of regular whole milk. (Follow the directions on the box.)

Meat filling: Meat filling for this is the same recipe for Rice Dressing, except add more meat. I add hot water if dry. See "Marie's Rice Dressing" recipe. Mix cornbread dressing and meat filling together well. Add green onions and put in a baking dish and bake on a low heat in the oven, or put in a dish on top of the stove in a hot water bath. Bon Appetit! Serving Ideas: Great for Sunday dinners and a must for the holidays.

FRESH OKRA, CORN & LIMA BEAN SUCCOTASH

Serving Size: 15

3 pounds okra - cut
1 pound lima beans
1 pound fresh or frozen corn
1 can crushed tomatoes

1 small onion - chopped
1 small bell pepper - chopped
2 pods garlic
1/4 cup oil

In heavy pot, cook okra and tomatoes for about 10 minutes in hot oil. Add all other ingredients and cook another 15 minutes. That's it!

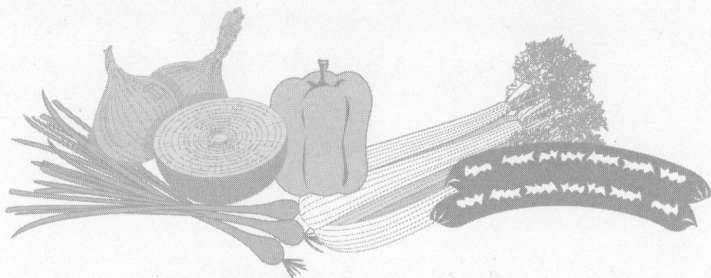

MARIE'S MEATLESS DIRTY RICE

Serving Size: 6

8 ounces water chestnuts - sliced
8 ounces mushroom stems & pieces
1 can french onion soup

2 sticks butter
1 large can chicken broth
2 cups uncooked long grain rice

Melt butter in heavy sauce pan. Saute drained mushrooms about 10 minutes (save juice from cans). Add french onion soup, mushrooms and water chestnuts. Add raw rice and mix well. Add seasoning to taste (very little salt). Put in covered baking dish and cook 45 minutes in a 300 degree oven. Stir or toss with fork after about 25 minutes. If it's dry, add a little warm water while tossing. Serving Ideas: Serve with meats or fish with tossed or fruit salad.

MARIE'S RICE DRESSING

Serving Size 15

2 pounds ground beef and pork
1 pound liver and gizzards
  boiled and ground
3 tablespoons oil
1 large onion - chopped
1 medium bell pepper - chopped

2 stalks celery - chopped
1 cup water
1 cup green onions, tops and
  bottoms - chopped
1 dash Kitchen Bouquet
3 cups long-grain white rice -
  cooked

Meat filling: Heat oil in heavy pot on stove. Brown meat well, season with salt, black pepper, cayenne, and Accent to taste. After meat is cooked, stir in onions, bell pepper, celery and garlic until wilted. Then add water and Kitchen Bouquet. Reduce heat and cook for appr. 45 minutes, stirring occasionally. In large mixing bowl or pot, combine cooked rice and meat filling. Mix well. Sprinkle with green onions. If dry, add a little oil. This meat filling can also be used for cornbread dressing. See "Famous Cornbread Dressing." Serving Ideas: Great for Sunday dinners and a must for the holidays!

AUNT LUCY'S SHREDDED CABBAGE

Recipe By: LUCY THIBODEAUX
Serving Size: 4

1 medium cabbage - shredded fine
1/2 med. bell pepper, red, julienned
1/2 med. bell pepper, green, julienned
1 medium onion - julienned
1 clove garlic - chopped fine

1/2 teaspoon salt
1/4 teaspoon red pepper flakes
1 dash black pepper
4 tablespoons oil

Place all ingredients in a medium size pan, perhaps a Magnalite. Saute on medium-high heat, approximately 10 minutes, stirring occasionally. Turn fire off and cover for another 10 minutes. This dish will make its own juice. Option: Raw shrimp can be added 3 minutes before you turn fire off. Bon Appetit! Suggested Wine: Nice Chablis. Serving Ideas: Serve over steamed rice.

GREASY GRAVY CHICKEN

Serving Size: 6

3 pounds frying chicken - cut
1/2 medium onion - chopped
1 bunch green onions - chopped

1/2 med. bell pepper - chopped
1/2 teaspoon minced garlic

Season chicken as desired. Brown chicken on all sides in heavy pot, then set aside. Saute onions, green onions, bell pepper and garlic for appr. 2 minutes in the same pot as chicken. Return chicken to pot, add appr. 1/2 cup of water. Reduce fire to low heat and let simmer for about 30 minutes. Serving Ideas: Serve over rice with vegetables of your choice.

MARIE'S CHICKEN SAUCE PIQUANT

Serving Size: 10

1 large hen - cut
1 large onion - chopped
1 large bell pepper - chopped
2 ribs celery - chopped

3 pods garlic - chopped fine
14 ounces tomato paste
8 ounces crushed tomatoes, canned
1 cup roux

Season hen pieces with salt and pepper. Put a little oil in a heavy pot, brown hen well, and remove. Put all other ingredients in pot, mix well and let simmer a minute or two. Return chicken to pot, add enough water to cover hen, let cook until it comes to a boil uncovered. When it comes to a boil, lower the fire and cover. Cook for 1 hour or until hen is tender. You may add green onions and parsley. I do! Serving Ideas: Serve over rice...Good eating!

MARIE'S PICKLED PORK AND BLACK-EYE PEAS

Serving Size: 10

1 pound black-eye peas
1 pound pickled pork
   parboiled, cut small
1/4 small onion - chopped

1/4 medium bell pepper - chopped
1 pod of garlic - chopped fine
1 stick oleo
6 cups water

Parboil pickled pork and put aside. Wash and put beans in pot with the other seasonings. Season with salt and pepper to taste, easy on the salt. Then add 6 cups of water, add pork and 1 stick oleo. Cook on low heat for about 45 minutes. Add water if you think it needs more water. It should be juicy to go over rice. Serving Ideas: Goes well with smothered seven steaks.

PORK FRIED RICE

Serving Size: 5

1 pound pork steak
  cut in 1 inch cubes
1 cup rice, long grain - cooked
1 medium onion - chopped
1 medium bell pepper - chopped

2 pods garlic - chopped fine
1 rib celery - chopped
1/2 cup water
Soy sauce

Season meat with salt, black pepper, and cayenne pepper to taste. Cut pork and brown in heavy pot with a little oil. Add soy sauce, then all other ingredients, except rice. Cover and let simmer. Stir in rice, remove from heat and serve. Serving Ideas: Serve with green salad.

CALF'S LIVER A-LA MARIE

Serving Size: 6

2 pounds calf liver
1 medium onion - chopped
1 medium bell pepper - chopped
3 stalks green onions - sliced

2 pods garlic - chopped
1 tablespoon parsley, freeze-dried
2 tablespoons flour (Wondra)

Season liver with salt, pepper and Accent (optional). Sprinkle flour on one side. Brown liver in hot oil on both sides, add all other seasonings and a little water. Cover and let simmer on low heat for about 15 minutes. Serving Ideas: Very good with grits, rice or creamed potatoes.

MARIE'S SHRIMP (OR CHICKEN) & OKRA GUMBO

Serving Size: 15

2 lbs. shrimp or
1 large fryer (chicken)
  seasoned and cut
2 pounds okra, fresh
  cleaned and cut
1 large onion - chopped

1 medium bell pepper - chopped
1 stalk celery - chopped
1 can chopped tomatoes
2 quarts water
1/2 cup roux

Brown chicken pieces and put aside. Cook okra in a little oil (maybe 1/4 cup) so that the okra won't be so slimy. Add the tomatoes, onion, bell pepper, and celery, and cook another 5 -10 minutes. In another pot, bring 2 quarts of water and 1/2 cup roux to a boil. Stir often to prevent roux from sticking. After roux and water starts to boil, add chicken or shrimp and okra. Cook for at least 20 minutes longer. Serving Ideas: Serve in a bowl over rice.

MARIE'S STUFFED PORK ROAST

Serving Size: 25

1 large pork roast
1 cup garlic - chopped
4 medium green and
   red hot peppers - chopped
1 small bell pepper - chopped

1 small onion - chopped
1/2 cup salt
1/4 cup black pepper
1/4 cup vinegar
1/4 cup oil

Note: This will make a large batch of seasoning stuffing, use just what you need and save the rest for another time. (Store excess seasoning in a jar and refrigerate.) Mix the above ingredients well. Turn your roast bottom up and start making holes with your knife at a slight angle. Make about 8 or 9 holes and stuff seasoning in each hole. Then I cut small pieces of meat from the end of the roast and close the holes to keep the seasoning from coming out when you turn it over to stuff the other side. Don't cover the holes on the top. Be sure to stuff the top side also. Put roast in a heavy roaster with 1 1/2 inches of water in bottom. Cover and place in a 350 degree oven on bottom rack. Cook covered for 2 1/2 hours, then uncover for another 2 1/2 hours. Baste roast every once in a while. I also use this stuffing for turkeys and beef roast. Serving Ideas: Serve for special occasions and a must for the holidays.

SMOTHERED STEAK

Serving Size: 10

4 large chuck or 7-steaks
1 medium onion - chopped
1 medium green onion - chopped
1 medium bell pepper - chopped

1 tablespoon flour, (Wondra)
1 pod of garlic
1 cup water

Season steaks well on both sides. Brown in hot oil in a heavy pot on both sides, then set aside (leave the juice in the pot). Add onions, bell pepper, garlic and green onions. Saute for appr. 2 minutes. Dissolve flour in water. Return steaks to pot, add water and simmer (covered) for appr. 45 minutes. Reduce fire. For thicker gravy, add a little more flour and water mixture to pot. You can coat steak with flour, if desired. This recipe can also be used for smothered pork steaks. Serving Ideas: Serve over white rice with hot vegetables and salad.

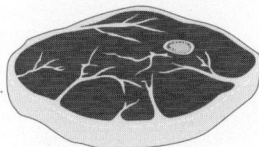

WEDDING TIME

Marriage is a sacred blending of two lives. During the ceremony, possibly, a tear may be seen on the mother's eye. This is a happy occasion as the father smiles as guests are welcomed to a reception honoring the couple. There will be music and dancing, delicious refreshments for all to enjoy. Marie places beautiful linens on the serving tables, silver trays and dishes amidst twinkling candles that cast enchantment for the occasion.

Treasured recipes that have proven favorites are presented in this section.

DEVILED EGGS

Serving Size: 24

1 dozen eggs - boiled
1 tablespoon sweet relish
1 teaspoon Worcestershire sauce
1 teaspoon lemon juice
3 tablespoons mayonnaise
1 tablespoon mustard

Boil eggs. Add a dash of salt to water. Peel and cut eggs in half, remove yolk. Mash egg yolks, add relish, Worcestershire sauce, lemon juice, mustard, and mayonnaise. Season with salt, red pepper and black pepper to taste. Stuff eggs and sprinkle with paprika. Serving Ideas: Everybody loves deviled eggs for the Holidays and parties.

MEXICAN BEAN DIP

Serving Size: 25

2 cans bean dip
1 medium avocado - mashed
1/2 cup lemon juice
8 ounces sour cream
1 package taco seasoning mix
Tabasco sauce
1 bunch green onions - chopped
2 large tomatoes - chopped
1 bar cheddar cheese - grated
1 bar pepper cheese white - grated
1 can black olives, pitted - sliced

Mix the following together and set aside; avocado, sour cream, taco mix, lemon juice and Tabasco sauce to taste. Mix the following in a separate bowl, green onions and tomatoes. Spread bean dip evenly in bottom of large serving dish. Top with avocado mixture, spread evenly over bean dip. Top with grated cheese, then top with onions and tomatoes. Top lastly with black olives. Serving Ideas: Dip with king size Fritos or other suitable chips.

PAT'S CRAWFISH DIP

Recipe By: PAT MORROW
Serving Size: 10

8 ounces cream cheese
1 package Italian seasoning
3 large eggs, hard-boiled, chopped fine
2 pounds crawfish - boiled
1 1/2 cups mayonnaise

Put cooked crawfish in food processor. Blend together all ingredients and chill. Serving Ideas: Serve cold with fancy crackers.

MARIE'S SWEDISH MEATBALLS

Serving Size: 25

2 pounds ground beef
2 pounds ground pork
1 cup herb-seasoned bread crumbs
2 large eggs

1/2 cup parsley flakes
2   small onions - chopped fine
1/2 cup water
1   bottle barbecue sauce

Soak bread crumbs in a little warm water. In a mixing bowl add all of the above ingredients and mix well. Make bite size meatballs and season to taste. Spray a cookie sheet and place meatballs on it. Bake in a 350 degree oven for 25 minutes. Then place in a warmer with your favorite BBQ sauce. Serving Ideas: Great at a social gathering. Serve with toothpicks nearby.

CRAB MORNAY

Serving Size: 40

2 pounds crabmeat - chunk
2 sticks butter
1 medium onion - chopped
1 medium bell pepper - chopped
2 stalks celery - chopped

4 tablespoons instant flour, Wondra
1 pint Half & Half
2 pods garlic - chopped
2 tablespoons parmesan cheese
1 shot sherry wine

Place crab in colander to thaw, let drain onto pad. Go through with fingers to check for shells. It is better to use real crab meat and not imitation.

Melt butter in heavy pot. Add celery, onion, bell peppers, garlic and flour. When bubbling hot, add Half & Half and parmesan cheese. Season sauce to taste. Reduce to low heat and let come to thickness desired. Let cook for approximately 5 minutes. Stir in crab meat and sherry wine, then remove from heat. Serving Ideas: Serve hot or cold. Serve with tart shells or fancy crackers. See tart shell recipe (page 33).

MY EASY SPINACH DIP

Serving Size: 15

2 10 oz pkg frozen chopped spinach
1 pound processed American cheese,
   jalapeno - cut in 1/2 inch cubes
1 cup milk

2 small onions - diced
2 2-ounce jars diced pimentos
   drained
2 medium tomatoes - diced

Squeeze spinach dry, set aside. Combine cheese, milk, onions, and pimentos in the top of a double boiler. Bring to a boil. Reduce heat to low, cook until cheese melts, then add spinach and tomatoes. Stir well. Serving Ideas: Serve warm with tortilla chips.

SPICY MEATBALLS

Serving Size: 20

50 medium rolled meatballs
1/2 bottle reg. size BBQ sauce
4 tablespoons ketchup

5 tablespoons brown sugar
8 ounces tomato sauce

Steam cooked meatballs. Add a little water in bottom of pan. Heat sauce and season with salt, black pepper, cayenne and Accent to taste. Put meatballs in serving dish, then pour sauce over them.

HOT BROCCOLI DIP

Serving Size: 15

2 8-ounce pkg. frozen broccoli
   chopped
1 small onion - chopped
1 small bell pepper - chopped
1 8-ounce mushroom stems and pieces
   drained

1 pound Velvetta cheese
1/2 stick butter
1 can cream of mushroom soup
   condensed

Steam broccoli, drain and put aside. Saute onions, bell pepper and mushrooms in butter. Add the cheese, broccoli and soup and simmer for about 5 minutes. You can use fresh broccoli. Serving Ideas: Serve with Melba toast.

TART SHELLS FOR SEAFOOD DIPS

Serving Size: 60

3 cups all-purpose flour
1 teaspoon salt
3/4 cup vegetable shortening, butter flavor

3 tablespoons parmesan cheese
1/4 cup milk

Mix the above ingredients well. Make small balls and pat into small muffin tins. Bake in a 325 degree oven for about 15 minutes. No longer. They should come out golden brown. Let cool before taking them out of muffin tins. Serving Ideas: Serve with dips such as Crab Mornay Dip...Crawfish Dip, etc.

ALICE'S CRAWFISH AU-GRATIN

Recipe By: ALICE MORROW
Serving Size: 25

4 tablespoons butter
2 bunches green onions
    top & bottom - chopped
4 tablespoons all-purpose flour
1 cup whipping cream
1/2 cup white wine
1 teaspoon salt

1 teaspoon red pepper
1 teaspoon Tabasco sauce
1/2 teaspoon garlic powder
12 ozs Mexican jalapeno cheese,
    Velvetta
6 ounces Swiss cheese - grated
2 pounds crawfish tails

Saute onions in butter for appr. 6 minutes. Add flour, cream, wine, salt, pepper, Tabasco, and garlic. Cook on high 6 more minutes. Stir cheese into hot mixture until it is blended. Add crawfish and cook 12 minutes. Serving Ideas: Serve in chafing dish with assorted Melbas.

HOLIDAY PUNCH

Serving Size: 20

2 cups cranberry juice cocktail
2 cups orange juice
1/4 cup lemon juice

1/2 cup sugar
1 1/2 cups white wine - chilled
1 bottle champagne

Combine juices and sugar. Stir until dissolved, then pour in punch bowl. Add wine and champagne and decorative solid piece of ice. Serving Ideas: Serve during holidays or any special occasion.

MARIE'S WEDDING PUNCH

Serving Size: 100

96 ounces pineapple juice
96 ounces orange juice
1 pint real lemon juice

2 cups sugar
1 gallon water
2 large strawberry Kool-aid

Heat water and dissolve sugar, then add the above. Make ahead of time and freeze in plastic gallon bags. Take out of freezer 4 hours before serving time. Make an ice mold to float in punch bowl. Add one bottle of ginger ale or Sprite to each punch bowl. Serving Ideas: Great for any social occasion.

MARIE'S OPELOUSAS MEAT PIES

Serving Size: 24

2 pounds boneless pork,
   Boston butt
2 pounds boneless beef,
   stew meat
2 pounds boneless chicken
1 small can green beans
1 small can corn

1 small can peas
1/2 cup roux
1/2 medium onion - chopped
2 stalks celery - chopped
1/2 medium bell pepper- chopped
3 stalks green onions, tops and
   bottoms -cut

Steam pork and beef until tender, then add chicken and steam another 20 minutes. Set aside and let cool, then chop in 1 inch chunks. In heavy pot, mix all ingredients. Add a little of the water the meat was cooked in. Salt and pepper to taste. Simmer about 15 minutes, it should be thick. Put in shallow pan and let cool. Sometimes I make it a day ahead, it handles better chilled. Serving Ideas: With a fruit salad, you have a full meal.

PIE CRUST FOR MEAT PIES

Serving Size: 24

5 cups all-purpose flour
6 teaspoons salt
3 cups oil

6 medium eggs
3 teaspoons baking powder
4 cups water

Mix eggs, water and oil, add to flour, salt and baking powder mixture. Mix well and make balls the size of golf balls. Roll out on a floured counter top. Have a pastry brush in a cup of water. Brush around the dough you've already rolled out. Put a spoon of filling in center, fold over and make moon-shaped pie, squeezing it down with your fingers, then use a fork all around the fold. Fry in deep oil until golden brown.

PARTY TIME

    The delectable flavor of the Creole "joie-de-vivre" is in the air. There is going to be a party! Neighbors from miles around will share in the musical happiness that comes from a homemade combo - an accordion, wash board, and metal triangle. This festivity is a "fais do-do." The families even bring the babies, hoping that they will fall asleep to the music.

    Dance, laugh, enjoy friends: this is the French-Creole way. The favorites of the "bon temps rouille" might be Jolie Blanc and Allons a Lafayette, to name a few. Furniture has been removed from the house, leaving plenty of room for the dancing and merrymaking. The teenagers are carefully chaperoned by the watchful eyes of Ma-Ma and Pa-Pa. Hopefully, the babies have been lulled to sleep by the music.

    The bountiful table adds to the enjoyment: popcorn balls, chicken gumbo, pralines, and lemonade. Marie invites all to the rhythmic party. Be her guest!

MARIE'S SHRIMP MOLD

Serving Size: 10

4 envelopes gelatin powder,
  Knox - soaked and put aside
1 pound shrimp - ground
3/4 pound Velvetta cheese
3/4 cup mayonnaise
2 tablespoons horseradish
3 tablespoons lemon juice
1/2 small onion - ground

1/2 small bell pepper - ground
1/2 rib celery - ground
3 tablespoons pimento - ground
1 teaspoon salt
1 teaspoon black pepper
1 teaspoon garlic powder
2 cups V-8 vegetable juice
1/2 stick butter

Peel and de-vein shrimp. Saute shrimp in one-half stick of butter, then grind in food processor, set aside. Then grind celery, bell pepper, onion and pimento...put that aside. In a heavy pot melt the cheese and the V-8 juice. When melted, add the Knox gelatin and all other ingredients. Refrigerate in a 5 cup mold overnight. Note: To unmold, I sit the mold in a little hot water and count to ten, comes out easily. Lay it on a bed of lettuce. Serving Ideas: Great for any socials. Serve with fancy crackers.

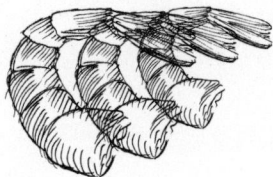

SPINACH DIP

Serving Size: 25

20 ounces frozen spinach - chopped - drain and pat dry
1 small can water chestnuts - drained and diced
1 package Knorr vegetable soup mix
1 pint sour cream
1 cup mayonnaise

Mix all of the above ingredients, season to taste, then place in a party dish and chill for appr. 3-4 hours. Serving Ideas: Serve with Toast rounds.

CRAWFISH DIP

Serving Size: 10

2 pounds crawfish tails, frozen
2 sticks butter
2 stalks celery - chopped
1 medium onion - chopped
1 cup water
1 small roll jalapeno cheese - cubed

1 medium bell pepper - chopped
3 tablespoons instant flour
  (Wondra)
2 pods garlic, chopped
1/2 bunch green onions, chopped

This is the same recipe for Crawfish Etouffee but for the dip we use less water and add jalapeno cheese. Place crawfish tails in colander to thaw, season well and set aside. Grind 1/2 of your crawfish in a food processor, set aside. Melt butter in large pot, add celery, onions and bell pepper. Saute until transparent; glazzy. Fold in crawfish and flour, saute 3 minutes. Add water slowly to thickness desired. Then add cheese, cook until melted down. Remove from heat, top with green onions. Place in warming dish or can be served cold. Serving Ideas: Serve in tart shells or with fancy crackers.

SPINACH MADELINE

Serving Size: 15

2 packages frozen spinach
  chopped - drain and pat dry
1 stick butter
4 tablespoons instant flour (Wondra)
2 tablespoons onion - chopped
1/2 cup evaporated milk

1/2 cup vegetable liquid
3/4 teaspoon celery salt
3/4 teaspoon garlic salt
6 ounces jalapeno cheese
  cut in 1 inch cubes
1 teaspoon Worcestershire sauce

Cook spinach according to directions on package. Drain and reserve liquid. Melt butter in saucepan over low heat. Add flour, stirring until smooth, do not brown. Saute onions slightly. Add liquid slowly, stirring constantly to avoid lumps. Cook until smooth and thick. Add seasoning (salt and cayenne to taste). Add cheese cubes. Stir until melted. Combine with cooked spinach. You can stuff inside monkey bread or bake in glass chafing dish with buttered bread crumbs on top. Serving Ideas: Serve hot or cold with fancy crackers.

STUFFED MUSHROOMS

Serving Size: 20

20 mushrooms, whole
1 small onion - chopped fine
1 clove garlic - chopped fine
1/4 cup bacon - crumbled

1/2 cup chicken - chopped fine
2 tablespoons chicken stock
3 tablespoons herb bread crumbs

Dig stem out of mushrooms and chop fine, saute stems, onions, garlic, chicken and crumbled bacon. Add chicken stock and bread crumbs to make a dressing. Season well with black and cayenne pepper. Stuff the above in the mushrooms. Cover with buttered bread crumbs. Then broil as needed, appr. 15 minutes. Serving Ideas: Serve as an appetizer for your next party.

JALAPENO SALSA

Recipe By: YOLANDA
Serving Size: 20

1 pound jalapeno - chopped fine
1 can tomatoes (Rotel)

1 can whole tomatoes - peeled
1/4 tablespoon parsley - chopped

Chop all of the above items and add garlic salt to taste. That easy! Serving Ideas: Serve with tortilla chips.

SPICY MEATBALLS

Serving Size: 20

50 medium rolled meatballs
1/2 bottle reg. size BBQ sauce
4 tablespoons ketchup

5 tablespoons brown sugar
8 ounces tomato sauce

Steam cooked meatballs. Add a little water in bottom of pan. Heat sauce and season with salt, black pepper, cayenne and Accent to taste. Put meatballs in serving dish, then pour sauce over them.

MARIE'S SOUTHERN GINGER BREAD

Serving Size: 20

1 cup sugar
1/2 cup oil (Crisco)
1/2 cup butter
1 cup molasses
2 teaspoons baking soda
1 cup boiling water
1 teaspoon cloves
1 teaspoon ginger
1 teaspoon cinnamon

2 1/2 cups flour - sifted
2 large eggs - beaten well
1 cup confectioner's sugar - sifted
3 tablespoons butter - softened
3 large egg yolks
1/4 cup boiling water
1 teaspoon lemon rind
3 tablespoons lemon juice

Ginger Bread

Sift flour and sift again with cloves, ginger and cinnamon. Cream Crisco and sugar, add butter then add molasses. Dissolve soda in boiling water and add to the sugar mixture. Beat until smooth and add the eggs last, beating well. Pour into greased 8 x 12 x 2 inch pan and bake at 350 degrees for 45 minutes or until done. Cut in squares.

Lemon Sauce

Sift the confectioner's sugar. Beat butter until soft, then add the sugar, gradually blending until creamy. Beat in egg yolks. Then stir in the boiling water, slowly cook over a very low flame until it thickens. Remove from heat, add lemon juice and rind. Pour over warm gingerbread. Serving Ideas: Serve gingerbread warm with lemon sauce.

THE RECIPE OF SOUTH LOUISIANA

Serving Size: 25

4 1/2 quarts Sprite
12 ounces frozen orange juice
6   ounces frozen lemonade

6 ounces lemon juice, concentrate
5 cups vodka

Mix Well. Very good! Serving Ideas: Pour over ice.

AUNT BEA'S CHOCOLATE CANDY

Recipe By: BEATRICE COLLINS
Serving Size: 20

3 pkg. chocolate chips, semi-sweet
1 pint marshmallow cream
1/2 pound butter
2 1/2 cups pecans -chopped

2 teaspoons vanilla extract
1 large can evaporated milk
  (Carnation)
4 1/2 cups sugar

Mix all ingredients in a large bowl except milk and sugar. DO NOT COOK.
In a large heavy pot add the sugar and milk. Bring to a boil, then continue
boiling for 9 minutes, stirring constantly. Then add this to the first mixture in the bowl and mix well. Pour into greased pan and let set in refrigerator two to three hours. Cut in squares. Enjoy!

BOBBY SAM'S PEANUT BRITTLE

Recipe By: BOBBY SAM
Serving Size: 15

1 3/4 cups light Karo syrup
1/4 stick margarine
2 cups unsalted peanuts

1 teaspoon vanilla extract
1 teaspoon baking soda
3/4 teaspoon salt

Bring sugar, syrup and margarine to full boil in a heavy pot, until it threads.
Add peanuts, cook until peanuts start to pop. Add baking soda, vanilla
extract and salt. Pour into greased pan.

QUICK PRALINES

Recipe By: ANN PORCHÉ
Serving Size: 12

1/4 cup water
2 tablespoons butter
1 cup brown sugar
1 cup powdered sugar
1 cup pecan halves
1 teaspoon vanilla extract

Mix brown sugar and powdered sugar together. Bring water and butter to a boil, add sugar combination and mix well. Bring mixture to boil and remove from heat after exactly 1 minute. Add pecans and vanilla extract. Beat until candy becomes dull (this doesn't take long). Drop by the teaspoon onto a cookie sheet covered with wax paper. Serving Ideas: The all-time favorite Louisiana candy.

MRS. FONTENOT'S PRALINES

Recipe By: MRS. FONTENOT
Serving Size: 20

1 1/4 cups sugar
3/4 cup brown sugar
1/2 stick butter

1/2 cup milk
1 teaspoon vanilla
2 cups pecan halves

Cook sugar and milk to a soft ball stage. Add butter; when melted take from fire and beat until it begins to thicken. Add nuts and vanilla. Drop a teaspoon at a time on wax paper. That's it.

MARIE'S LEMON BARS

Serving Size: 24

2 cups all-purpose flour
1 cup butter or margarine
1/2 cup powdered sugar

TOPPING
2 cups sugar
2/3 cup lemon juice
1/4 cup flour, all-purpose
1 teaspoon baking powder
4 medium eggs

Preheat oven 350 degrees. Combine flour, butter and powdered sugar, mix thoroughly. Press into well greased 13 x 9 inch pan. Bake 20 minutes.

Topping

On medium speed of mixer, mix eggs, sugar, salt and lemon juice. Fold in 1/4 cup of flour and baking powder. Pour onto hot crust, bake 25 minutes longer. Cool - cut into 2 inch squares and sprinkle with powdered sugar. Makes 2 dozen. Serving Ideas: Use as a dessert or for a finger food at a party.

MARIE'S DELIGHT

Serving Size: 12 - 14

3 envelopes Knox gelatin
1/2 cup cold water
1 angel food cake
  broken in chunks

CUSTARD
1 cup milk
6 egg yolks
1 cup sugar
2 chocolate squares
1/2 teaspoon salt
1 teaspoon vanilla extract
2 pints whipping cream

First Step: Soak 3 envelopes of Knox gelatin in 1/2 cup cold water. (Set aside.) Second Step: Take angel food cake and break into chunks. (Set aside.) Third Step: Heat milk on low heat for about 4 or 5 minutes. Beat egg yolks in sugar and salt, pour into scalded milk stirring constantly for about 3 minutes. Then add chocolate and gelatin and vanilla extract. Set aside to cool. Whip egg whites until stiff, then add 1/2 cup of sugar, a little at a time. Toss custard and egg whites into angel food cake and mix well. Pack mixture into Pyrex dish or square pan. Then whip two pints of whipping cream and spread over dessert. Sprinkle chopped pecans on top of whipped cream. Refrigerate overnight. When ready to serve, cut in squares. Enjoy!

CRAWFISH ETOUFFEE

Serving Size: 6

2 pounds crawfish tails
2 sticks butter
2 stalks celery - chopped
1 medium onion - chopped
1 1/2 cups water

1 medium bell pepper - chopped
3 tablespoons instant flour
(Wondra)
2 pods garlic - chopped
1/2 bunch green onions - chopped

Put crawfish tails in colander to thaw, season and set aside. Melt butter in large pot, add celery, onions and bell pepper. Saute until transparent, glazzy. Fold in crawfish and flour, saute 3 minutes. Add water to consistency desired. Let cook for approximately 15 minutes. Remove from heat and top with green onions. Serving Ideas: Serve over rice with salad and french bread.

CRAWFISH FETTUCCINE

Serving Size: 20

3 pounds crawfish tails
1 1/2 boxes fettucine noodles
  boiled
2 stalks celery - chopped
3 tablespoons instant flour (Wondra)
2 pints Half & Half

2 pods garlic - chopped
2 tablespoons Parmesan cheese
4 sticks butter
1 pound Velvetta cheese - cubed
1 medium onion - chopped
1 medium bell pepper - chopped

Boil fettuccine by following directions on box. Melt butter in heavy pot. Add celery, onions, bell pepper and garlic. Add flour. When bubbling add Half & Half and Velvetta cheese. Season to taste with salt, black pepper, cayenne and Accent. Reduce to low heat. It will be thin, don't worry. Mix fettuccine and sauce, pour into baking dish. Sprinkle Parmesan cheese on top. Bake for approximately 30 minutes in moderate oven (350 degrees). Serving Ideas: Serve with green salad and garlic bread.

LOUISIANA FILLETED CATFISH WITH MUSTARD BUTTER SAUCE

Serving Size: 2

3 cups cabbage -thinly sliced
1 1/2 tablespoons dijon mustard
1 tablespoon white wine vinegar
1 tablespoon dry sherry wine
3 catfish fillets

1/2 cup milk
1 cup flour - seasoned for dredging
1/2 cup vegetable oil (Lou-Ana)
4 tablespoons butter
3 bunches green onions, thinly sliced

Blanch the cabbage in salt water for 2 minutes. Drain and transfer to a platter, keep cabbage warm. Mix together the mustard, wine and vinegar in another bowl. Dip the filleted catfish in the milk and dredge in seasoned flour. In a heavy skillet, heat the oil over med-high heat, saute fillets, turning once cooked...about 3 minutes. Transfer and arrange on bed of cabbage. Wipe skillet clean, then melt the butter on med-high heat until light brown. Add the mustard mixture. Pour sauce over fish, garnish with green onions.

MARIE'S SEAFOOD GUMBO

Serving Size: 15

5 pounds shrimp
  peeled and de-veined
2 pounds crab meat
1 medium onion - chopped
1 medium bell pepper - chopped
3 stalks green onions

1 rib celery - chopped
1 tablespoon garlic - chopped
1/2 stick butter
1 pint roux
5 1/2 quarts water

Saute the above ingredients, except for green onions, shrimp and crab meat, in the butter for 5 minutes. Then add 1 pint of your choice of roux and the water. Salt and pepper to taste. Cook on low heat for appr. 45 minutes, then add the shrimp and cook for about 15 minutes, then add crab meat and green onions. Remove from heat. Serving Ideas: Serve in bowl over white rice with green salad or potato salad.

MARIE'S CATFISH AL-LA-BOURRAY

7 1/2 pounds catfish fillets
1 1/2 sticks butter - melted
2 pounds shrimp
1/2 bag bread stuffing
1 small bell pepper - chopped

1 small onion - chopped
1 stalk celery - chopped
2 pods garlic - chopped
1 bunch green onions - chopped

Stuffing

Saute the shrimp in butter. Chop half of the shrimp. Put the other half aside. Saute all of the vegetables and add the chopped shrimp and bread stuffing along with the green peppers. Add water to soften. Salt and pepper to taste.

Catfish

Cut fish in serving size pieces. Cut pockets into each piece. Fill with the stuffing mix and place in pan or dish.
Take the other half of shrimp and season. Sprinkle shrimp over fish along with 1 1/2 sticks of melted butter. Pour a little lemon juice over fish and bake in the oven at 400 degrees for 35 - 45 minutes. Spoon sauce over fish every once in a while. Serving Ideas: Serve over my dirty rice, with a salad and bread. Enjoy!

This catfish dish started without a name. I received a request from a group of fifteen men to prepare a fish supper to be served at a card game. I purchased 7 1/2 pounds of catfish, and I wasn't sure how I was going to prepare it. I came up with a great idea for the fish and here is the recipe.

When the supper was over, the group of men wanted to know the name of this dish. I told them that there wasn't; it was something I created off the top of my head. The players of the Bourray game decided to call the mystery dish MARIE'S CATFISH AL-LA-BOURRAY. The rest is good eaten'!

NANA RUTH'S EGGPLANT A LA CREOLE

Recipe By: RUTH SAMIERE/Riverside, CA

Serving Size: 4

1 1/2 cups eggplant - cubed
1/2 cup onion - chopped
1/2 cup green pepper - chopped
1/2 cup celery -chopped
2 tablespoons bacon fat

1 large tomato - diced
6 slices bacon
1 cup crumbled crackers
1/2 stick margarine

Soak eggplant in salt water for 30 minutes, then cook in boiling water until tender. Fry bacon, then brown green pepper and onions in bacon grease. Add tomatoes and eggplant and season with salt and pepper to taste. Place in casserole dish, crumble bacon and sprinkle over eggplant. Then add melted butter and sprinkle with crumbled crackers. Bake in a 350 degree oven for appr. 25 minutes.

NANNY'S CHICKEN MEXICOLA

Recipe By: RUTH SAMIERE
Serving Size: 6

1 fryer - cut in serving pieces
1/2 cup flour (Wondra)
1 teaspoon sugar
2 teaspoons salt
2 teaspoons black pepper
1/4 cup oil

2 medium onions - chopped
2 medium green peppers - chopped
16 ounces tomato sauce
1 cup chicken broth
2 teaspoons chili powder

Coat chicken with mixture of flour, sugar, salt and pepper to taste. In deep heavy skillet, brown chicken in oil. Remove chicken, then saute onions and bell peppers until tender. Add tomato sauce, broth, chili powder and chicken, cover and simmer about 40 minutes or until chicken is tender, on a reduced fire. Very good! Serving Ideas: Serve over rice with a salad.

MARIE'S LOUISIANA CORN AND CRAWFISH

Serving Size: 10

1 can whole kernel corn
1 can cream style corn
1 stick butter or margarine
1 small can chopped tomatoes
1 small onion - chopped
1 small bell pepper -
   chopped

1 tablespoon sugar
2 tablespoons all-purpose flour
2 pounds crawfish tails
1 stalk celery - chopped
1 tablespoon garlic cloves

Saute onions, bell pepper, celery, garlic and flour in melted butter or margarine about 5 minutes. Then add crawfish and remaining ingredients, lower heat, and cook for another 10 - 15 minutes. Serving Ideas: Serve as a main dish over rice.

THE PASSING

The older one gets, the faster the days of life skip by. God-given life is a wonderful gift. In this created world we are given eyes to behold beauty and ears for the enjoyment of sound. Touch and taste enhance the adventure of life. One door may close, but another opens. It may be termed the "passing" or the other "shore." – in colloquial French "le morte."

Marie's heart beats in love for those in these circumstances. The bereaved family and friends gather after the requiem Mass to remember the days of the departed and to encourage each other for the coming days. It's never good-bye, but "au revoir."

The table is laden with delectable food as life must go on. The following recipes are but a token of Marie's love and concern.

MARIE'S FAMOUS CHICKEN SALAD

Serving Size: 30 sandwiches

2 pieces of breast of chicken
  and 2 pieces of dark meat
3 boiled eggs
1/2 stalk of celery
1/2 small onion
1/2 small bell pepper
2 tablespoons diced pimento

2 tablespoon parsley flakes
Salt and pepper to taste
3/4 cup mayonnaise
2 tablespoons mustard
3 tablespoons Kraft salad dressing
3 tablespoons sweet relish

Boil chicken until tender, cool and cut in chunks. Run through food processor for about 30 seconds, then put in a bowl. Run eggs through food processor, then celery, onions, bell pepper, and pimento until they are pureed. Add remaining ingredients to this mixture, then add to chicken. Mix all ingredients well. Very good! Serving Ideas: This recipe can be used as a salad on lettuce cups or make sandwiches with it. Note: This is for 1 quart. One quart will make 30 sandwiches.

AUNTIE'S POUND CAKE

Serving Size: 15

1 pound butter
  melted and beaten
1 pound sugar

12 eggs
1 pound all-purpose flour
2 teaspoons vanilla extract

Mix above ingredients well. Pour in greased bundt pan. Bake at 300 degrees for 1 hour or until toothpick comes out clean.

GLAZE

Mix 1 cup of sugar, 1 teaspoon of almond extract and 1/2 cup of water in a small pot. Cook for appr. 5 minutes, then remove from heat. When cake comes out of oven and while hot, brush glaze over cake using a pastry brush.

DATE NUT CAKE

Serving Size: 15

2 sticks butter
1 cup sugar
2 cup all-purpose flour - sifted
4 medium eggs
1 teaspoon baking soda

1 pound dates - chopped
1/2 pound cherries - chopped
4 cups pecans - chopped
1 teaspoon vanilla extract

Cream butter, add sugar (blend well), stir in sifted flour and baking soda. Add eggs, dates, cherries, nuts and vanilla extract and mix well. Pour into ungreased tube pan and bake in a 300 degree oven for 1 1/2 hours. Remove from oven when done and invert immediately.

MARIE'S CHICKEN DELIGHT

Serving Size: 6

3 cups chicken, cooked
   cut 1/2 inch thick
1 pkg. wild or white rice - cooked
1 can cream of celery soup
1/2 cup bell pepper, red and green - chopped

1 medium onion - chopped
2 cans french style green beans - drained
1 cup mayonnaise (Hellmann's)
1 cup water chestnuts - diced

Mix all ingredients together. Pour into casserole dish, then bake appr. 25 minutes at 350 degrees. Toss once with fork after 10 minutes or so of baking. Do not cover. Easy as that! Serving Ideas: Serve with salad and bread.

AUNT LUCY'S BROCCOLI & CAULIFLOWER CASSEROLE

Recipe By: MRS. LUCY THIBODEAUX
Serving Size: 10

1/2 medium cauliflower
3 bunches broccoli
  cut into flowerets
1 stick butter
3 tablespoons all-purpose flour

2 cups whole milk
1 medium onion - julienned
2 cloves garlic - chopped fine
3 cups mozzarella cheese - grated

In a medium size sauce pan, season 1 1/2 cups of water with half an onion, garlic and salt, black pepper and cayenne to add flavor when steaming. Steam cauliflower for about 10 minutes then place broccoli on top, steam another 5 minutes. Drain and put aside. Mix on low heat, butter and flour. After mixture has dissolved, then pour in milk and whisk. Add salt, black pepper, and cayenne to taste. Add the other half of onion and cheese to sauce. Cook until bubbling, then remove from fire. Butter 9 x 13 inch casserole dish and layer cauliflower on one side and the broccoli on the other. Pour half of the white sauce on top and sprinkle 1 cup of grated cheese. Layer again and pour the remaining sauce and cheese on top. Bake in a 350 degree oven for about 30 minutes. Serving Ideas: Serve with any meal.

MARIE'S FAMOUS POTATO SALAD

Serving Size: 15 - 20

5 pounds red potatoes
7 medium eggs
  boiled and chopped
2 stalks celery - chopped
1 small onion - chopped

1/2 cup pimentos
1 cup mayonnaise
1/2 cup Miracle Whip
1/2 cup sweet relish
2 tablespoons mustard

Boil potatoes until tender. Cool, peel and dice. Add all of the above ingredients. Season to taste with salt, black pepper and cayenne pepper. Add more mayonnaise, if needed. Mix well. Bon Appetit! Serving Ideas: Great with Sunday dinners or Bar-B-Ques.

CHICKEN/SAUSAGE JAMBALAYA

Serving Size: 25

6 medium chicken breasts
  cut 1/2 inch thick
2 pounds sausage (Pork)
  cut 1/4 inch thick
1 medium onion - chopped

1 medium bell pepper - chopped
1/2 bunch green onions - chopped
2 pods garlic - chopped
1/2 cup oil
4 cups rice- cooked

Cook rice and set aside. Boil chicken breasts in 3 cups of water for appr. 20 minutes. In another pot, boil sausage slices in 3 cups of water for appr. 20 minutes. Save chicken broth to be returned to Jambalaya. Season chicken cubes. In heavy pot, saute onions, bell peppers, and garlic in oil on stove top. Add chicken and sausage, saute appr. 5 minutes. Add chicken broth, reduce to low heat and cover completely for 15 minutes. Mix in cooked rice. Place in serving dish, then sprinkle green onions on top. Serving Ideas: Serve with green salad or cole slaw and french bread.

CHICKEN/PORK JAMBALAYA

Serving Size: 25

3 pounds pork
6 medium chicken breasts
    cut 1/2 inch thick
1 medium onion - chopped
1 medium bell pepper - chopped

1/2 bunch green onions - chopped
2 pods garlic -chopped
1/2 cup oil
4 cups rice - cooked

Cook rice and set aside. Boil chicken breasts in 3 cups of water for appr. 20 minutes. Save chicken broth to be returned to jambalaya. Season chicken cubes. Saute onions, bell peppers, and garlic in oil on stove top in heavy pot. Add chicken and pork and saute appr. 15 minutes. Add chicken broth to chicken and pork, reduce to low heat and cook for 15 minutes. Mix in cooked rice, place in serving dish. Sprinkle green onions on top. Serving Ideas: Serve with green salad or cole slaw and French bread.

MARIE'S CHICKEN & SAUSAGE GUMBO

Serving Size: 15

1 7-pound hen (not fryer)
    cut in four
1 pound pork and beef sausage
    sliced

1 small onion - chopped
2 pods garlic - chopped
1 small bell pepper - chopped
1 1/4 cups roux

First, I get the butcher to cut the hen in four. I wash it well and season it with salt and pepper, then I put it boiling in a gallon and a half of water. When tender, I cool it and take the meat off the bone, except for the wings, I cut them in half. Cut the rest of the meat in bite size pieces. In the broth the chicken was boiled, put in the five other ingredients, add more water, if needed. Let cook another 10 - 15 minutes. When done, I add green onions and parsley. Serving Ideas: Serve over rice.

MARIE'S STUFFED PORK ROAST

Serving Size: 25

1 large pork roast
1 cup garlic - chopped
4 med. green and red hot peppers
   chopped
1 small bell pepper - chopped

1 small onion - chopped
1/2 cup salt
1/4 cup black pepper
1/4 cup vinegar
1/4 cup oil

Note: This will make a large batch of seasoning stuffing, use just what you need and save the rest for another time. (Store excess seasoning in a jar and refrigerate.) Mix the above ingredients well. Turn your roast bottom up and start making holes with your knife at a slight angle. Make about 8 or 9 holes and stuff seasoning in each hole. Then I cut small pieces of meat from the end of the roast and close the holes to keep the seasoning from coming out when you turn it over to stuff the other side. Don't cover the holes on the top. Be sure to stuff the top side also. Put roast in a heavy roaster with 1 1/2 inches of water in bottom. Cover and place in a 350 degree oven on bottom rack. Cook covered for 2 1/2 hours, then uncover for another 2 1/2 hours. Baste roast every once in a while. I also use this stuffing for turkeys and beef roast. Serving Ideas: Serve for special occasions and a must for the holidays.

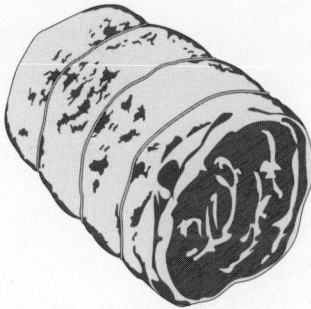

INDEX

SOUPS & SALADS

BEVERAGES

DESSERTS

CASSEROLES

SEAFOOD

VEGETABLES AND SIDE DISHES

MAIN DISHES

ORDER FORM

Marie's Catering
~~819 W. Park Avenue - Opelousas, Louisiana 70570~~
~~(318) 948-3726~~

Website: ~~www.creolerecipes.com~~
E-mail: ~~creoleladybug @email.com~~
creoleladybug2000@yahoo.com
11038 Slate River LN Houston TX 77089

Please send_____copies of "Mais Oui Marie, Creole Cookin"

at $9.95 each $ _____

+$2.00 *250* per book for shipping and handling $ _____

Louisiana residents add sales tax ($.80 per book) $ _____

Total Enclosed $ _____

Name _____

Address _____

City, State, Zip _____

Phone _____

Please enclose check or money order payable to Marie's Catering.

Allow approximately 2-4 weeks for delivery.

FAVORITE RECIPES

Recipe Name   Page No.

_____

_____

_____

_____

_____

_____

_____

_____

_____

NOTES

_____

_____

_____

_____

_____

_____

_____

_____

_____

_____

_____

_____